Where The Wings BREAK AND RISE

Hiya Banerjee

BlueRose ONE.com
Stories Matter
NewDelhi • London

BLUEROSE PUBLISHERS
India | U.K.

For permissions requests or inquiries regarding this publication, please contact:

BLUEROSE PUBLISHERS
www.BlueRoseONE.com
info@bluerosepublishers.com
+91 8882 898 898
+4407342408967

ISBN: 978-93-7139-449-9

Cover Design: Aman Sharma
Typesetting: Pooja Sharma

First Edition: June 2025

CONTENTS

AMIDST THE ADRENALINE RUSH

It's frightening,
The thought of losing you.
I believed I knew the art of things changing,
But I guess it's just something you never get used to.

Eighteen and polished,
I need to leave even if I don't want to.
There are things I must explore,
Dreams that I have to realize and pursue.

But even amidst this adrenaline rush, lies a small fear,
I don't want to move too far away from you.
You are everything I hold dear,
You are the person I value.

I trust your words,
I know you will stay by my side.
But I am still scared to let go,
What if our bond turns out to be treaded and dried?

Yet, I can't let this feeling control me,

The future keeps calling me.

I have to move forward,

I have to be courageous enough to leave everything behind and head northward.

While I move to the next step of my journey,

I still hope that you and I pause for a minute.

When we are thirty and worthy,

I hope we still confide in each other without any restraint or limit.

INDELIBLE NOTES OF THE PIANO

She glanced at him again.

She couldn't help it,

He was so alluring that she couldn't take her eyes off him,

However, she knew that it would never last longer than a minute.

His laugh was always so merry,

But she knew it was reserved for another.

She had sketched his eyes over and over in her secret diary,

But she kept it to herself as she watched him lock his fingers with his precious other.

Why did he have to be so kind?

Why did he accidentally have to touch her fingers when they played the piano?

She couldn't have him so she wondered,

'Why couldn't he have been shallow?'

She never thought of foiling his happiness,

All she ever wanted was to admire him from afar.

She knew that to him her feelings would seem bizarre,

She knew that he was a faraway star.

So, she continued playing the piano with him,

One song and the next.

Until she only remembered him as a beautiful hymn.

Years passed by, she looked back upon his warmth as a fond memory,

Never wanting to forget;

He was her first love,

Complex yet ever so perfect.

HIRAETH

If I had to choose a place to go to,
It would be a home;
A home where everyone bickers yet it feels warm,
A home where everyone's emotions are unharmed.

Some place where I won't have to hide in a corner,
And bawl my eyes out.
Some place where I meet a gentle reformer,
Who strengthens my heart.

A home where laughs are louder than nonsensical chatter,
Where everyone disagrees but still sticks around.
A home where scars heal,
With a single apology, even if it is confound.

An abode which is sometimes infuriating,
Yet the most altruistic place.
An abode which welcomes my flaws with arms wide open,
Only to embrace.

MY BREAKTHROUGH

Laughing with you,
It's past 4 AM already.
I can't even remember when we started chatting,
Maybe at 11 PM?
Maybe I don't even care now that my spilling thoughts are steady.

You have this unimaginable effect,
I can't even explain.
Who are you?
Oh right, you are my best friend.
In a world full of lies, someone I can at least call mine,
A friendship that leaves a good taste like a fine old wine.

Did you know your smile is contagious?
Spreading like a disease,
It makes my face beam with giggles,
Before you I hadn't met someone who hadn't put me through complex riddles.

It's fun now,

I can finally say it out loud.

I have you and I know you love me too,

My only last selfish wish is to stay with you.

I beg for it to be true,

After all you are my break through.

And now that you are here,

I have a feeling that you are not just a passing wind that blew,

But a sturdy ship that will stay even beyond my mess and strew.

THE ESCAPE TO THE COUNTRYSIDE

Abused, suppressed and tattered,
I wanted to run away.
Without a trace, Without a clue,
To a place with vibrant colours and a beautiful view.

So, I did.
I ran away to the countryside,
The news of the lord's missing daughter,
Spread like a wildfire, countrywide.
They say, the daughter of the Marquess was nothing but unrefined.

The whole empire rustled and bustled,
They thought I was already dead.
I mean, how could a spoiled daughter of a noble survive without her expensive bread.

Little did they know that I had been saved.
This farmland, at the corner of the continent,
Set my wings free which had long been enslaved.

I, who, once drank fragrant flower tea,
Was now fond of drinking warm milk by the sea.
The etiquette lessons long forgotten,
I was now a free woman, who had escaped the capital whose crux itself was rotten.

While I worked towards my independence,
The gossip was nowhere to be found, all cleared;
Like every other high society's social subject that was hot only for a moment before it disappeared.

My scramming, too, had been buried with time;
But it was no matter,
As they were the ones still stuck in the dusted era while I broke through the docile lady they had created,
Earning more than just some dime.

THE NEXT CHAPTER

Things have been hard and rough,
I have often been forced to swallow.
But right now, I am choosing;
Choosing to focus on things I can control,
Choosing to sort my problems today instead of waiting for tomorrow.

I judged myself too much,
Everyone's views were a burden to follow.
But at this moment,
I choose to create a life of intentional happiness and comfort over something materialistic and hollow.

I have been broken and damaged,
I was a coward to not overcome it.
But recently I have dealt with the chaos calmly,
Uprooting the negative seeds and planting new ones filled with better memories;
The havoc; averaged.

Today, I decided to step into the next chapter,

Leaving behind all what ifs.

Erasing the manipulations instigated by a captor,

Flipping the coin on every turn and accepting my scars as my gifts.

I WONDER WHY?

It feels tiring,
Always giving but never even receiving a smile.
It feels piercing,
The way you put them above and call me the one with the guile.

I picked up,
Whenever you called me.
I became the grown up,
Whenever you needed something comforting.
Yet, I was the one treated the worst,
It felt like an act of invisible buffeting.

When I bared myself and showed my teardrops,
You declared me a fop.
When I cried out for help,
Your harsh, rude words made my heart drop.

It made me wonder,
Why don't I have someone whom I don't have to ask to treat me right?
Why do I always have to be the one to fight with all my might?
Why don't I have a friend who will make me their highlight?

I wonder why?

Even when I try so hard,

Even a hug is difficult to find.

I wonder if it will all stop,

When I stop trusting them like a blind.

THE STORMS IN MY HEAD

In the pitch-black darkness,
I search for a light,
A light that belongs to me and only me;
I could smell a scent but no candlelight.

I touched the broken glass,
Yelling in the musk.
But it only echoed,
And went around coming back as a brusque.

Negative, Negative, Negative;
My thoughts grinned like a devil,
I was unwanted, unwanted, unwanted;
It was a tactic to lure a drevil.

And I fell for it over and over,
The belief was deep rooted.
The insecurity lingered like a hangover,
My future was thus, concluded.

So I drowned in them,

Until nothing was left in my eyes

They were blank and sombre,

I stopped struggling,

Just like their scheme which had been viciously devised.

IN THE PAGES OF AN AUTHOR

Pushed and slandered;
A fragile soul who always forced herself to feign,
In reality she is a coward who only ever knew how to swallow and abstain.

But in her mind, she is everything that she can't be;
A female knight,
In a world of aurora nights,
Someone who does not give up before a fight.

In that world; elsewhere,
She has both the thought and the thew;
She is a powerful princess in a society,
Where the dim-witted princes knew nothing but labelling witty women as shrew.

She is only but an author.
Weaving her words carefully,
Wanting to be a part of her imagination;
Drafting it viscerally.
She inks it beautifully,
Leaking her deepest desires;
Sharing it universally.

THE LIBRARY'S SHELVES

My head on her lap,
I was young and immature,
I remember my mother telling me,
"Souls don't meet by accident",
It sounded all so pure.

Seventeen and confused,
My only allure was the library,
Until I crashed into you.
They said soulmates find each other,
And like a clichéd story, I found myself staring at a non-existent hue.

I met you again,
I didn't realise we were in the same class.
Who are you?
I felt an attraction,
And for the first time I couldn't argue.

A boring girl,
Sitting in a quiet corner of the library;
Yet, you glanced at me.
But I was lost in the books,
Between the lines, daydreaming and carefree.

You finally talked to me,

You needed my help.

A book recommendation?

Do you even read?

For the first time,

I witnessed you willingly enter my solace,

The beautiful world of books;

The library.

It was like a storyline,

Where the boy with a huristic approach,

Fell for the girl who was lost inside the world of myths;

The perfect catchline,

Weaved by a wordsmith.

At the thought of it,

I could feel my skin tingle,

It was a sign that a new chapter was beginning.

A slow romance was the plot this time,

For I could hear the library's shelves mischievously grinning, giving away a sweet tinkle.

I FELL FOR YOU AND I'M STILL FALLING

Your amber eyes,

Caused a strange pounding to arise.

The time slowed down,

I heard the clock's countdown.

I never craved attention,

But I wanted a taste of yours.

I couldn't name this tension,

Even your voice reassures.

Crush, like or love;

I didn't know yet,

Words, beauty or something above;

I unknowingly imagined myself looking down at you through the lunette.

I became a dreamer and you became my dream,

Your hand in mine,

I never saw a future for this daydream.

That crinkled smile,

I can't believe as I walk down the aisle;

Tying the knot with an unbreakable thread,

The easiest "yes" I've ever said.

I still act tough and deny it all,

But the truth is that,

Beneath the sun's warmth;

I am still endlessly scrawling.

In the past and now,

I fell for you and I'm still falling.

A COLD NOVEMBER NIGHT

A cold November night,
I was sitting on a call;
Telling you all my crazy stories,
The funny incidents echoing through the walls,
Oh, what an unforgettable moment of nightfall.

We are miles apart,
Yet your comfort was close
That telepathic connection,
I tend to forget all my woes.

Your clumsiness;
And my never-ending talks;
We are just over sharers,
Our secrets hidden behind screeching chalks.

You believe in forever,
I never believe in the concept of lifetime,
Yet we walk shoulder to shoulder,
Watching each other shine.

It's been six years now,

That sounds too long.

But in 'just' six years,

Your brave heart gave my sensitive soul a place to belong.

"BURNT CREATIONS"

Sometimes I wonder,

Where did it go?

The literature, the culture, the originality that we used to highlight with a profound glow.

We call ourselves a proud citizen of this nation,

But are we really?

When all we do is look at others, following their directions;

Burning and killing the crest of our own creations.

The classics, once known to all,

Now known to none.

The plays, once replayed,

Digged and buried inside a grave;

Unknown, cold and idly laid.

I wonder again,

If we will realise;

The meaning behind our novelty?

If we will finally come to accept,
Our own identity.
If we will ever stop destroying,
Our everlasting works of art filled with nothing but pure creativity.

SIBLINGS' AGREEMENT

It's already been too long;
You are twenty-two and I am seventeen,
Are we still hiking together?
Are we still hiking along?

The bond we share,
It's still the same, for now
Are there going to be differences?
Are there going to be topics in the future where we disavow?

Doubts,
Filling up my head.
Tomorrow scares me,
But I guess I am geared up to bet.

I will take the chance,
Gambling across the room,
Not even sparing a glance at the space rising like brume.

I will reside in the present,
Where everything is about what we do,
What is the point in probing?
Thinking about how far I can be the childish me with you.

So, let's laugh together while we can,
Let's continue living in the siblings' agreement;
Where fears come and keep leaving,
The deal always backing up, despite our playful disagreements.

"I ACCEPT, I'M SENSITIVE"

I could say, "I'm sensitive",

But I'd rather not.

Hiding this fact,

Playing it cool,

All of these just make my chest feel odd.

I went through my memories;

The strong and weak ones,

And then I finally came to a conclusion,

Doesn't everyone get sensitive sometimes during their long runs?

Everyone cries,

They all laugh along,

They all make diverse memories that are to be remembered lifelong.

A different situation,

Brings out a different hurt.

A different event,

Brings out a unique happy blurt.

We all have our moments,
The blues and colourful hues,
That makes us experience that single word.
And this makes me wonder again,
Isn't being sensitive better than being left unstirred?

And so I accept, I am a sensitive girl,
Who dreams big,
But bawls her eyes out,
When an episode takes a sudden whirl.
But I also know that I am one of those girls,
Who sits to have a secret private affair,
With all her emotions,
A delicate self that tends to freely unfurl.

UNMASK IT

I am trying hard,
One. Two. Three.
Repeat.
I am working for hours,
Only to plunge down the muddy steep.

I am stepping up,
One stair at a time.
It's a rusty touchup,
I fall back from my prime.

I grab onto the ropes of hope,
Bruising my palm, a different colour of despair.
I feel like a nobody who has lost all her scope,
And is beyond any repair.

A weird darkness covered my heart,
My artistry trapped in a casket.
My desires were ripped apart,
Inner voices yelled, but my eyes shined with a sudden brightness,
Whispered the secret message; "Unmask it".

The envoy forced me back on my feet,

Reminding myself,

My dreams were too big to die incomplete.

Started counting again from twelve o' twelve,

My win was racing nearer;

Outshining the discontents of my unfriendly cliques.

LIKE A GIRL WITH A HIGH SCHOOL CRUSH

Looking at her,
oh, she is so in love.
Like a girl with a high school crush,
her foot was completely fixed in his foot glove.

She sounded so excited,
talking to me.
It was all about him —
I could hear it in her voice;
she was in for a passionate swim.

All she spoke of,
was how simple he made her feel.
I was tiny bit envious,
but the affectionate smile on her face
made my emulative thoughts crumble under the wheel.

She squealed,
and I listened.
"He has the prettiest eyes!"
was all I heard for weeks.

I am happy for her;
happy for him.
He is the answer to her question —
"Who will be the one to treasure me beneath my act of prim?"

I hugged her — my best friend —
knowing that her wish came true,
That he looks at her when she looks away to see the view.
My heart still yearning for something similar,
but for now, her joy is mine,
while I patiently wait for my very own cue.

BEHIND A WALL

What if I told you the truth?
That I am scared —
scared of everything.

That I tremble when I hear about the future,
but I hide it well behind a wall.

That I smile brightly,
even when everything in my mind is a mayhem.

That I am full of positivity,
even though I am scared to expect.

That I am hurting,
but insist on resisting well.

That I am unsure,
if someone else believes in me too.

That I am wavering,
but in the end,
still commit to be strong and true.

SOLD DOWN THE RIVER

She was her best friend.
She didn't comprehend,
what was going to become of them.
She never knew they were bound to condemn.

Her best friend didn't understand;
what she felt.
She endured with a sombre expression,
But had she really knelt?

No, she craved revenge;
she wanted satisfaction to heal her ache.
She craved to see her companion break.

She stayed by her side as a fake.
Spreading rumours,
uncovering her secrets,
pitying her just for namesake.

She laughed resembling the devil.
She destroyed her confidant's life.
She swiveled the knife,
her mouth spitting venomous lies.

Her best friend was left defeated.
She still didn't know what she did wrong.
All she knew was that it was her day one,
who had denounced her all along.

WITHERED FIERY PETALS

Dear Roses, on my cherished book,
the pages that I wrote dried up with you.
The fragrant flowers were now,
bleeding against the thorns,
the spike; a grappling hook.

Dear Roses, on my favourite chapter,
What happened to you?
Your fiery red petals,
have lost its sense of valor,
forsaking the residue.

Dear Roses, the one that lives in between my journal,
How long have you been dead?
I wish to replace you with a fresh one now,
but I can't seem embrace the feeling of these fallen flowers,
who have already met their end.

THE TEA, STAINS

The tea stains so be careful when you spill.
Everything, everywhere connects;
Beware of the momentous thrill.

The walls have ears,
the skin feels fears.
Don't forget that the stain might be the reason for someone's tears.

You never know the chapter that you skipped,
might be from the book of lies.
The ink written by an overdramatic
author;
wearing a disguise.

So be careful when you uncover the plot.
Life is a game,
the narrative might be a mere fire to the flame.
When the levity strikes the clock,
the cue will fit in the keyframe.
And everyone shall muse on;
the mystery that had once brewed in that teapot.

ATHYMY

Can I just talk to someone?
Please?
I can't figure this out alone.
It is something outside what I can do,
I should've known.

Can someone please help me?
I don't know how I feel.
I seem to be losing my touch,
losing my zeal.

Please, please, please.
I feel numb.
Nothing feels right,
my thoughts are in a stifling fight.

My eyes are growing cold.
My heart is becoming icy.
I can't feel a thing,
hypnotized and trapped in the vines of a poisoned ivy .

ROSE GOLD

A rose gold light,

different than I had ever seen.

Lilies blooming in my heart,

this was the first time I have ever witnessed such a scene.

Is this what they call love?

When the nights are bright with stars,

When the summer light gleams through the rough?

When every guitar string strikes "ours",

Is this love?

Little space between us,

I can communicate well.

This feeling feels ridiculous.

This solicitude rings dangerous,

but my inner spirit can't help but dwell.

Those three words, "I love you",

didn't know they would light up my heart.

Our whispered rendezvous,

didn't know those mumbles would paint my castle rose gold
even on its rampart.

EXTINGUISHED WRANGLE

"Quiet!"
But I don't want to!
Thought that my voice will be my sword,
But it was just a fantasy;
too good to be true.

"Just listen!"
But why do I have to?
Forcing your opinions on me,
dragooning me into engraving my shackles like a tattoo.

"Shut your mouth!"
Who said I need to?
My words crumbling,
but there is nothing wrong from your point of view.

"Shush!"
Am I obliged to?
My beliefs do not matter.
My empty words just keep repeating the same,
through and through.

WRITTEN IN RUNES

I never felt that I belonged anywhere.
I sit inside my own head,
just a blank slate —
a rune carved: "nowhere".

Irritating. Disgusting. Anger.
Words that bind me to the 'offender's' chair —
wicked melancholy,
confining me from everywhere.

Booming mocking laughter.
A place crammed with slanderous affairs —
blaming me for all the misdeeds,
voices leading me to despair.

Maybe in another time,
I would at least belong somewhere.
Flower gardens would be flumping in my mind,
following the alley down,
to "anywhere".

MOTHER'S WARRIOR

Crying and crying,
Until you come to me running.
You pick me up and hug me tight,
I hold your fingers with my little hands,
"My daughter",
you say with a smile.
This feeling felt just right.

Fell down the stairs,
you ran over immediately.
My eyes only know tears,
"Shh, my daughter", you say as I listen obediently.

Just thirteen,
tortured by emotional waves.
Anger. Anger. Anger.
My words are as harsh as a glaive.
You still smile warmly,
couldn't analyse your face,
until you finally hold my hand firmly,
"My daughter is worthy."

Now seventeen,

I am mature and wise,

but I still hold onto your hand tightly —

because the warmth never dies.

I want to be just like you.

I wish to make you happy.

I want to engrave something that is nothing but true.

I want you to read it out loud proudly —

The stories of a soldier.

She isn't just her father's princess,

She is also her mother's warrior.

To my mother

MUCH HAS CHANGED

When did we grow up?
I didn't even realise.
From being at each other's every round up ,
to not being available at my worst cries.

From holding my hand when crossing the road,
to not being there when I walk through those difficult cross roads.

I wonder where did all those flamboyant seasons go?
Our childish crimes,
those healthy times,
where your funny poetries would always rhyme.

Your provoking words that were always directed at me,
your baiting lies that I always believed to be true.
Your fake expressions filled with glee,
never changed into nothing new.

Your weakness?
I still don't know.
You are perfection to me —
you only inspire me to grow.

NOT ONCE, NOT TWICE.

No matter how much I forgive you,
how can I forget?
those hateful words,
that slip out as if they are nothing but regret.

You repeat the same sentences,
not once, not twice,
but again, and again.
Making me feel guilty,
for something I never did.

Your words are like a sharp sword,
hurting me in places even I didn't know exist.
They hurt my feelings deeply —
as if I was paying back a debt,
as if I was always the first choice on your blacklist.

You say things so easily.
You don't even think beforehand,
how much they make me ache,
or how much they might affect.
The smile I stretch forcefully is wounded bland.

It is normal to you,

a line, a word you say every day.

I get it; that to you I am a burden,

to you, I have always been a regret.

JUST THE WAY I DO

I care for someone,
who cares for me,
understands me,
drags me away from the deep sea.

I care for someone,
who prioritises me,
who scolds me,
when I scorn myself for nothing,
and tend to become edgy.

I care for someone,
who accepts me,
my talkative self,
and a hidden side I show hardly.

I care for someone,
just the way I do.
Someone who rejoices in my joys
Someone who is proud when I succeed.
Someone who has chosen to never misinterpret my deeds.

I care for someone,
who loves me;
genuinely —
no matter how immature or
extreme,
my behaviour can be.

I care for someone,
whom I will always care for.
Who will be my rock,
even when they don't know.
Who will hold my hand firmly,
no matter where I go.

PUNISHMENT METED

I have forgotten the feeling of when I used to be greeted.
This house, this room —
so empty and ceded.

Why was I so conceited?
My family, my children,
all left me saddened,
all this happiness that I caused to be deleted.

A mistake I made —
not once, not twice,
always repeated.

I was excused time and again,
but the warnings were unheeded.
Until the moment finally came,
when their sufferance exceeded.

I was running after fame,
aspired to be undefeated.
I failed to notice,
that my hard-won success meant nothing,
when my joy was already long weeded.

-Hiya Banerjee

EFFERVESCENT YOUNG POETRY

She resides in the poetry she cannot write.
She lives to the best,
with no fear ; no fright.

Vibrant colours are all she sees,
kindness surrounds her like a refreshing breeze.
She has a smile that reaches to her eyes,
always pretty and wise.

Her existence itself is a divine blessing,
upon this selfish world.
She is an elegant dressing,
so rare, so loved ,
someone who is deserved.

SEALED BOOK

I have anxiety,
but why must it interfere?
Why must it decide for me?
Why must it give me that hateful glare?

I am not someone who is disliked,
then why am I so scared?
Maybe because my deepest regret is;
I never dared.

I never dared,
to expose myself to someone who cared.
I reckoned my deepest feelings to always remain unshared.

When did I, an open book fall into this despair?
When was it,
that my lungs fell short of air?

In the end, didn't I do this to myself?
The anxiety and the fear —
it has always been me, constraining my pitiful self in this square.

I am the one who gave up easily,

ignoring it even though I was aware.

My stomach churned queasily,

I knew it was I, who treated me unfair.

I must open this book once again,

Read the pages

And find ways to attain,

A better me,

A chapter that shall break me free from the chains of this sorrowful abstain.

NIGHTED

Atone for your sins,
yes, you must.
For you have slaughtered your kin,
shattered the trust.

Suffer deeply,
as you must.
Destruction shall engulf you completely,
it will prove to be just.

Bathe in blood,
you must.
Since your hands are covered in a murderous flood,
your soul is promised to be ruined from its very crust.

PSYCHOMACHY

It breaks my heart to see you cry,
you look lonely —
you must've received too many goodbyes,
your eyes look cold and stony.

Your whimpers make me sad,
you are hurting.
Your sobs are trapped in an ivy clad,
your tears keep burning.

Your unspoken feelings,
fall like a river.
Your empty eyes stare at the ceiling,
while your tender hands constantly shiver.

I gather courage,
as I take a hold of them —
your trembling hands.
I pass my warmth,
to encourage.

Mother, I love you, I say.

Your eyes ignite,

as your footing finds the bay.

You come out of the plight,

ceasing it all,

you attend me.

But your eyes were still at war,

never finding a chance to be free.

LAST IN THE QUEUE

You all hurt me equally but maybe I shouldn't take it all so seriously?

but it pains —

pains my heart when you leave me alone,

leaving me on my own,

leaving me lonely,

making me break apart slowly,

Is it alright if I stay longer?

Is it alright if I try to make our bond stronger?

You don't seem to care anyway,

you just keep painting me grey.

Is it okay if I say —

say something that makes my day,

but it just feels wrong to share it

that way.

You act like you want me to stay,

but the next moment you want me away.

What should I do?

I don't understand —

Everything seems blue,

but maybe nothing you say is true.

Maybe I should just accept,

that I am just last in your queue.

DECAYING AWAY

One day when I go away,
I want to hear them say —
"You were braver than the others".

One day when I fade away —
I want them to look at me proudly,
not in dismay.

One day when I break away,
I want them to apologise,
for all the delay.

I wait for them eagerly,
but they never come.
I am sure they are spending their time somewhere leisurely,
as I lay there numb.

THE SECOND ALTERNATIVE

I don't think I know what it's like to be someone's first choice.
I have been a replacement, I have been a revoice,
but never a choice.

I am desperate —
desperate to be a friend,
desperate to loved,
desperate to blend.

It is not a thought.
It is fact —
a fact that makes me overwrought.

I am not someone who belongs,
I am someone who prolongs,
prolongs the moments lived by others,
prolonged in different shades of colours.

I am not someone's first choice,
the proof is my drowned voice.
I am a replacement,
The evidence is my sinking jumboize.

-Hiya Banerjee

DYED RED

I fell in love.
Enough to be drunk,
enough to make my heart funk.

I found something.
Something that makes me flutter,
something that burns sweetly like summer.

I rejoiced.
Painted a memory,
painted a love that was oh so heavenly.

I looked forward to the future.
Wrote a story,
a story filled with our glory.

I fell in love.
Until it all fell down,
until I lost my crown and tore up my white gown.
I dyed it red,
and dug a thorn in my chest as he bled.

I am no longer in love,

there are only buried feelings,

and lonely eyes that are still screeching.

ROSES AND GALAXIES

Forever is an illusion,
they say repeatedly.
But when I see you,
why does my heart beat unceasingly?

When our eyes meet,
when I dive in deep,
when I sense your feet fleetingly,
it is so sweet.

I feel your aura;
roses and galaxies.
The sensation lights up stars in me.

I feel your love,
a universe full of doves.
A spring that I have never seen,
the fondness colours my world in a beautiful green.

INSOUCIANT

Pierced my heart,
you doubted me.

A pitch-black art,
I had never foreseen.

A complexity;
playing in continuous scenes.

An emptiness;
filled up to never convene.

WILD HEARTS

Wild hearts don't break —
they await,
await to be burned with passion,
with the flying flames.

Wild hearts seek an affair,
but never in search of fames.
They wish to be rare,
extremely extraordinaire.

Wild hearts are the enthusiastic ones,
the ones who always jump the guns.
They are the sort that are always shunned,
but they are also the ones who would shine the brightest under the sun.

FOREORDAINED

You are a weapon,
you are a knife.

You are aggression,
always the one to strive.

You are a lesson,
a chapter; that is unbound and wise.

You are an expression;
destined to shield all the smiles.

The intercession,
who is shaped to be the future's eyes.
A justice who is fated against the lies.

INHUMANE

Blood on my hands,
as I kill myself and tear myself apart.
Deep scars with my fangs,
as I break my heart.

I destroy myself ,
splitting my core completely .
I break violently —
breathing in,
the air of melancholy.

I end my humanity,
and shatter my sanity.
I become a chaos ,
crushing my soul with brutality.

THE ECCEDENTESIAST

Free to be me,
it is what I wish to be.
"No pain, no agony";
is this thought itself a felony?

My laughter echoes,
but why does my heart still feel an unknown sorrow?
Maybe it knows,
knows how my loved ones caused me to choke.

My trusted left me wounded,
made me believe my true self was not needed.
He made me descend the throne I had found,
threw me away and left me hell bound.

My heart throbs,
reminding me of the stain.
I am no longer laughing
the feeling of wanting to be free is once again; collapsing.

SCIAMACHY

Marcid with war,
she stood there yonderly.
Once again, she was haunted by voices,
which echoed continuously —
"I HAVE CHOSEN THEE."

Her eyes were empty.
Her existence was druxy.
She was long gone in her own abditory.

She was like the marmoris,
drowning in the ocean.
Asking for no help,
not even trying to get sober.
She was a warrior of the cursed —
a legend whose mind was damned to interspersed.

FILIPENDULOUS

If I were to jump out of this window,
I wonder if I would finally be free?
Break through these rules and escape this cursed authority.

If I really jump out of this window?
Will I at least be dead?
Will I be able to tell the demons?
My dreams of the undead.

Now I am standing in front of this window —
ready to jump beyond and beneath,
ready to welcome afterlife,
ready to pay for my sins and deeds.

TALE OF THE BROKEN QUEEN

The story about a fierce queen was told in the kingdom of Maureen.

Betrayed by her lover,

Chained by her father,

she was a queen who was tamed by her mother.

Her past was an armour,

and it made her more of a monster.

She knew she wasn't born to be soft and quiet,

she was born to make the world shatter.

How did that sweet little girl turn into a horrid creature?

That is what her people wonder.

But what they do not know,

is that the sweet little girl was sealed away a long time ago after the death of her beloved brother.

MY SCARS

I hate my scars.
They remind me of how broken I once was,
when you left unveiling all my flaws.

I hate my scars.
They remind me of your strong yet suffocating arms,
of all your lies and fake charms.

I hate my scars.
They remind me of how much of a sham your words "it's alright" were,
how you put on a manipulating smile and said you love me with your every fibre.

I hate my scars.
They remind me of your bewitching eyes,
and how those eyes would just watch my wrecking body while I let out my sobs and cries.

But I love my scars.
because they taught me how to love again,
when you purposefully drowned me in the champagne.

I love my scars.

At least these scars never left me alone midway,

it helped me climb up to where I am today.

A THOUSAND FEELINGS

She is a simple person who hides a thousand feelings behind the happiest smile.

She is a person who acts mature,

but from inside she is just a child.

Her smile looks unbreakable,

like never cried.

But if you look closely, you can see the sadness in her eyes.

She feels alone in a room full of people.

She just wants someone to hug her,

someone who will burst the suffocating bubble.

She didn't know how broken she was.

Every time she wanted to laugh,

she just ended up crying so fast.

Her mind is overfilled with unsaid things,

and her heart is full of broken strings.

She is 'just' a simple girl who hid her broken wings.

SHE

She is a girl who smiles so bright.
She is a girl who loves to shine.
She is someone who is always kind.

She is someone who I can never be —
someone who taught me how to be truly free.
She always held me nearby and close,
She is the one who cherished me the most.

She assured me,
told me I had a shoulder to cry on when others saw me as their pawn.
Everyone backed off, but she used the word 'we'.
To the closed doors of my heart —
she became the key.

BLUE

I was trying to be strong,
but everything felt wrong.
I was trying to stand on my own two feet,
but all I feel now is empty and incomplete.

I took years to recover,
you knew everything yet you made me suffer.
I felt betrayed,
you used to be the first one to my aid.

You were a friend whom I trusted,
everything dropped down from the perfect hundred.
To me you were exemplary,
now I see you as a passing memory.

You thought you were being bold,
but my dear friend,
not anymore.

I cried enough and now your chapter is closed.
Thanks to you, I decided to be selfish,
I decided to be the one whom I cherish.

And maybe I did do wrong to you,
but I really want to forget it all and start anew.
Besides, someday you will realise it too,
some wounds will forever remain blue.

WHY ME?

If you ask 'why me'?
Does that mean you are unhappy today?
Maybe today you treated yourself too harshly.

You know that they will never care,
you know it but you still think your life is unfair.
You keep doubting what mistake you made,
you keep forgetting how they cut you down with the blade.

You cry a lot thinking that everything will be better the next day,
but you realised it doesn't work that way.
The next day gets worse because your eyes brim with tears,
you keep remembering that no one cares.

You always end up walking towards the mirror —
smiling bitterly.
You hate yourself so much,
the rage makes you quiver.

You disregard the days when you rush down the stairs happily.
Without a fail you run into his arms,
he is the one who keeps you safe from this brutality.

He is your brother;

your anchor.

He replaces your tears with giggles,

he is the one who treats you so well with no trace of any rancour.

You feel so lively around him,

he is the light in your grim.

So, in these moments of gaiety,

why do you fail to ask 'Why me'?

SMOOTH SAILING

Sometimes I wonder,
Do people hate me?
Do they need me?
Everything around me makes me want to flee,
I end up questioning myself 'Can I ever feel free?'

I get a sense of insecurity.
Is it too much to ask for a real friend?
Is it too much to want a sense of surety?

I waited and waited for a true friend.
A friend who will understand my pain,
a friend who will comfort my emotional blain,
a friend who will be loyal and never feign.

I was going to succumb to my fate,
when she had me at checkmate.
She showed me that things could change,
she showed me that I could rewrite that awful page.

Now I have gained courage,
I am not afraid of failing.
She was the soothing salve to my ailing,
my initial hiccups have found it's smooth sailing.

A GENTLE WARNING

I wanted to become beyond compare,
to show the people who treated me unfair,
that even I could reach somewhere.

I changed myself and over and over,
I was afraid of becoming nothing but a pushover.
Till I was swept away by what they said,
their whispers were widespread.

It was until one day I came to realise,
no matter what I say they will never feel suffice.
So, I will make sure that this time I won't be vandalized.

Now I only consider it a bad dream,
I won't fall prey to your scheme.
I want them to know that my future isn't something they can decide,
this is a gentle warning to let them know that the old me has died.

HYPOCRITE

Believe in yourself,
A tagline I say.
But do I believe in myself?
My thoughts stop midway.

'Such a hypocrite.'
I think to myself.
Who am I to say those words when I, myself tend to quit?

My mind struggles,
it wants me to keep going.
Everything seems exhausting.
Thus, I block my own vision,
trapping myself in my handcrafted prison.

I stretch a smile,
lie to everyone —
'Faith in yourself can you help you reach that one last mile'.
I pretend all the way through,
my positive words are vile.

MY HEART IS A SECRET KEEPER

My heart is a secret keeper.
Every time I gaze into your eyes,
the connection only gets deeper,
I always look back twice.

Everything between us is unspoken,
yet it all feels so loud.
A beautiful magic,
the million tiny butterflies make me squeal aloud.

When you smile,
all I can think about is "Oh Shit, can he ever be mine?"
You are so phenomenal,
every moment around you feels divine.

My heart is a secret keeper,
it has been dancing alone.
It doesn't know how to tell you,
about the seeds of love that you have sown.